Silly Jack
and the
Dancing Mice

Written by
Malachy Doyle

Illustrated by
Alexandra Colombo

"There's no food," said Jack's mum.
"We need some gold. Go and sell Daisy!"

At the market, Jack saw a man. The man sang, his bee played the harp and his mice danced.

Wow!

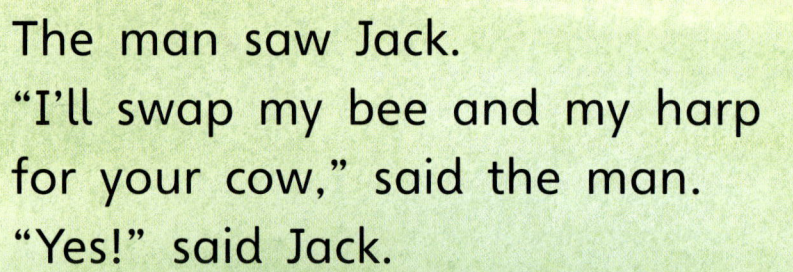

The man saw Jack.
"I'll swap my bee and my harp for your cow," said the man.
"Yes!" said Jack.

"These are no good, Silly Jack!" said his mum.
"We need food! Now we need to sell Rosie!"

Jack took Rosie to the market.
The singing man was there again.
He sang, his mice danced and
the crowd danced too.

I wish I had some dancing mice!

"I will swap my mice for your cow," said the man.
"Yes!" said Jack.

Jack's mum was NOT happy. "Come back when you have some gold!" she said.

Jack went off with the bee, the harp and the mice. He sang to cheer himself up. The bee played the harp and the mice danced.

Soon, lots of people were dancing too!

"The king will make you rich if you make the queen dance," said an old lady.

So Jack went to see the king.

Jack sang, the bee played the harp, the mice danced and people danced too ... but not the queen.

Jack got up on the table and did a very silly dance.

Then the queen got up on the table ...
and she danced too! The king gave Jack
a lot of gold.

"Am I silly now?" asked Jack.
"No," said his mum. "You are the **BEST**!"